NO, STOP, THAT'S NOT OKAY!

I0180939

Written By Kathy Tarpley

Illustrated By Aneeza Ashraf

ABOUT THE AUTHOR

Kathy Tarpley has an adult disabled child; her current passions include writing children's books and wildlife photography. She lives with her family in Gulf Breeze, Florida.

Thank you for reading my story. I look forward to reading your review, so please take a moment to post your thoughts on Amazon. You can also reach the author at freefall32536@yahoo.com.

Author-Kathy Tarpley (Facebook)
Author Central(Amazon)

Kathy Tarpley's Exceptionally Special Series

Exceptionally Special: I'm Deaf
Exceptionally Special: I'm Blind

A bully shoved me down today, then laughed at me, and walked away. If a bully shoved you down at school, what do you think you should do?

Should you chase them down and start a fight or shove them back; no, that's not right.

Instead with a firm voice, say, NO, STOP,
That's not okay!

Bullies love to see you cry, so smile and look them in the eye.

If a bully laughs and calls you names, say whatever, and calmly walk away.

If the bully continues to bother you, ask your teacher what you should do?

Also, tell your mom and dad; it helps to talk if you feel sad.

Bullies will point; they will whisper and stare.

They might grab your shirt or might pull your hair.

They might try to trip you as you are walking by,
Knock stuff out of your hands and hope that
you will cry.

They will do whatever they can to make you feel
scared, They will make fun of your shoes
and clothes that you wear.

Bullies are mean; they enjoy knowing you hurt,
They hope that their actions will destroy your
self-worth.

Stay away from the bully as much as you can, If you have to be near them, then first make a plan.

PLAN

1) Stay in group of friends.
2) Don't play alone.
3) Don't walk home alone.

Stay in groups with your friends, so you are never alone.

Don't play by yourself or walk home on your own.

There's not much reasoning with bullies, although you can try, Stay confident, strong, and hold your head high.

You have done nothing wrong, don't believe what they say. Try to ignore them and walk calmly away.

You Are:

LOVED

WANTED

NEEDED

SPECIAL

KIND

WORTHY

STRONG

AMAZING

CONFIDENT

PERFECT